CAVIES

(Guinea Pigs)

Cavies, or guinea pigs as they are more popularly called, make delightful pets. The author, in charge of a Zoological and Botanical Gardens at Ashover, Derbyshire, has bred these charming and remarkably fascinating animals for many years. With chapters on housing, feeding, breeding, showing, health and sickness, and the many varieties of Cavy, his invaluable book tells the reader all he would wish to know about their care and upbringing.

General Editor: W. A. FOYLE

CAVIES

(Guinea Pigs)

by

C. H. KEELING, F.Z.S.

W. & G. FOYLE LTD.

119-125 CHARING CROSS ROAD

LONDON, W.C.2

Reprinted 1972
© *W. & G. Foyle Limited, 1961*

**Printed in Great Britain
by Rocastle, Leavesden, Watford, Herts.**

TO ALFIE

In gratitude for many things

ACKNOWLEDGEMENTS

My thanks are due for the kind help and co-operation of the British Museum of Natural History, Manchester Museum, 'Fur and Feather', and Mr. Walters, late of Derby; also to my wife, who provided most of the illustrations, both line and photographic, as well as correcting the manuscript and dealing with all the correspondence attendant upon the production of this book.

Contents

List of Illustrations

CHAPTER ONE

Something about Cavies

I HAD NEVER felt so hot and uncomfortable in my life. Perspiration trickled irritatingly down my face and neck, while my near sodden shirt crept further and further upwards until most of the lower half of it seemed to be twisted round my waist and merely added to my misery. My feet felt as though they had been turned to lead, and with each painful step my thoughts wandered further away from my quest and hove nearer to glorious visions of shady trees and iced drinks. I was primarily doing this for you, my reader, as I was seeking the wild ancestor of the subject of this book, the Restless Cavy of the Andes of Peru. I had made a special journey to the British Museum of Natural History in South Kensington on one of the hottest days in the hot Summer of 1959 to see if they had a mounted specimen there whose description I could jot down and give here.

I happen to be one of those peculiar, and apparently rare, individuals who intensely dislike hot weather and in consequence made a most unpleasant journey to the Museum, only to find that they had no such specimen there and just very brief details about the domestic Cavy's evolution from it in a German scientific paper, printed about the year 1900, which I was not allowed to bring out. This was a pity because my German is limited to a sort of 'emergency vocabulary' of about 150 words and even then is of the pidgin variety, so as was to be expected I did not progress very far with it with no dictionary to refer to constantly. I left feeling disappointed, hot, tired, dusty.

longing for the Derbyshire hills I had left so hopefully that morning – and very little wiser about the origin of the Cavy. On the way home I mentally collected all the data I already had on the subject, which was really precious little and roughly as follows.

When the first Spanish conquistadors reached the Western side of the South American Andes in what is now Peru during the sixteenth century they found the strange, now extinct, race of people known as the Incas and, kept by them as pets, large numbers of small animals which I suppose they likened to Rats. These were Restless Cavies (*Cavia cutleri*) which were kept in a more or less domesticated state and might now be regarded as the only actually living relics of a dead race. The first specimens to be seen in Europe probably arrived about the year 1580 and were introduced by the Dutch, who doubtless obtained them from their colonies on the Guiana coast on the North-Eastern tip of the South American continent where they had been transported across mountains, rivers and vast forests from their distant homeland. Because of the name of their country of embarkation they were at first known in Europe as 'Guiana Pigs' but, as words are living things and have a habit of changing, this later became the now familiar 'Guinea Pig', the origin of which puzzles many people. As far as is known the first specimens to be seen in this country arrived about the year 1750, although no one seems to know just who introduced them.

As far as I can gather the Restless Cavy is roughly the size of his present-day descendant but is uniformly coloured greyish brown which, rather surprisingly, does not appear to be present in any of the modern domesticated varieties. It would appear that he was not really scientifically described until as late as the last century, when he received his scientific name in honour of an American naval officer who accompanied the great

Charles Darwin in his historic voyage in H.M.S. Beagle to the coasts of South America and the Galapagos Islands; just how he merited his name going down for posterity I do not know – perhaps it dawned upon him that no one had looked really closely at an animal which had been known for three centuries, so he suggested to the scientists that they might do so. The scientific name of the domestic Cavy, incidentally, is *Cavia porcella* which means 'Pig-like Cavy', although I can't think why. The various types of Cavies will be dealt with in a later chapter but it will suffice at the moment to say that they are many and varied. This makes all the more surprising the mystery of how they have evolved from the original wild ancestor, for no one seems to know very much at all on this subject. Like Topsy, the domestic varieties have apparently 'just growed' and I cannot help feeling that there is plenty of scope in this particular field for some enthusiastic zoological investigator – in short one might almost say that the history of the Cavy as we know it is shrouded in mystery, and as far as I can gather very little research has been carried out in this direction.

But let us have a look at a domestic Cavy.

It belongs to the great Order of Rodents, or mammals which gnaw, and as such is characterized by an ever-growing set of incisor teeth which are shaped not unlike miniature chisels and have to be kept at a suitable length by constant chewing of hard substances, especially wood, and by general wear and tear against each other. Sometimes a mouth injury or some similar minor mishap may cause one tooth to be pushed slightly out of line from the rest and the result may well be a grossly overgrown member which might eventually assume some fantastic formation if it does not cause its owner's death from starvation first. Occasionally Rats, for example, have been found dead because a lower incisor has grown upwards over the face like some grotesque fencing mask, described an arc, and eventually pierced the wearer's skull. In Cavies, however, the teeth do not seem to grow at quite the rapid rate that those of some other members of the Order do, which is certainly a blessing where the woodwork of their cages is concerned.

Although they have no connections whatsoever with the Ungulates, or hoofed animals, male Cavies are known as boars and the females sows, as in Pigs, and this is doubtless due to their rather puzzling popular name, which is still very widely used. A large adult boar measures some ten inches in length and might weigh as much as two pounds although the sow is usually considerably smaller and rarely attains this size. The body is cobby with a high rump, the legs short, and I always think that, when viewed in silhouette, the head is not unlike that of a miniature Sperm Whale, while the very sparsely haired ears are somewhat like those of an Asiatic Elephant – which makes this little creature sound a veritable *multum in parvo*. Other peculiarities are four toes on the forefeet as against three on the hind ones, and what appears to be a complete lack of tail; perhaps this latter characteristic is worthy of special comment. Mention to any ten people that you keep Cavies and I guarantee that nine of them will immediately fire back 'Oh, yes, if you pick them up by their tails their eyes will drop out', and then expect you to laugh – although if only they could hear themselves saying it they would soon desist. Actually the laugh is rather on them as these animals indeed have tails, although hardly in the accepted sense of the word; run your finger down a Cavy's spine towards where the tail should be, and at the base of it you should be able to feel, under the skin, a piece of bone which is shaped almost like a tiny arrowhead. This is formed by about five minute vertibrae, or bones, and is actually the root of what used to be quite a respectable tail which, for reasons which are by no means clear, started to disappear eons ago and has been absent for many centuries; evolution, however, is always on the move and in a few thousand years time even this queer internal nether appendage will have been lost.

Most Cavy books declare that the cry of the animal is a series of grunts and squeaks, but I can only suggest that the writers have never really listened to their subject, for although the sounds mentioned are often given vent to, by far and away the most frequently uttered cry is a very definite and clear 'wink, wink, wink', which has a surprisingly far reaching note and is so characteristic that my father always used to call these animals, facetiously, 'Winking Pigs'.

Perhaps the strangest thing about the Cavy, however, is the story that it never sleeps, although this is an extremely debatable matter and one which has not so far been solved: yet the name of its wild ancestor may be significant in this direction – think of it, *Restless* Cavy, which surely implies something along these lines although no one seems to know with anything like certainty. Where this little mystery is concerned, all I can say with anything like authority is that during the summer of 1956 I had occasion to visit the Zoological Gardens at Dudley in Worcestershire and there noticed a white Cavy, which to all intents and purposes was fast asleep and which seemed most indignant on being awakened when I investigated this unheard-of phenomenon.

When it first comes into the world the Cavy is very different from the Rabbit or Rat in that it is fully formed and well able to take care of itself. This is because in the wild it would live on the open grassland all its life and scorn such places of refuge as holes or burrows; obviously the young of such a race would have to be able to keep up with the rest of the nomadic colony from the very beginning in order to avoid enemies.

CHAPTER TWO

Housing

WHEN ONE BEARS in mind that keeping Cavies is very much like keeping Rabbits it will be seen that the housing of them is quite a simple matter, but please, please, make their cages of far more generous dimensions than those in which most of the latter animals are obliged to spend their cramped lives.

The ordinary type of Rabbit 'hutch' is almost ideal for Cavies; in fact the only thing against it is this matter of size, or rather lack of it. To house a pair of adult animals I suggest their cage be some 3 to 4ft. in length with a width of some 18 to 20in. and although the height is not so important I suggest it be nearly that of the width. The framework struts can be of $1\frac{1}{2}$in. $\times$ $1\frac{1}{2}$in. or 2in. $\times$ 2in. timber, and the actual bodywork of tongued and grooved boarding, while the front should be faced with either $\frac{1}{2}$in. (or 1in.) wire netting; anything larger than this could perhaps be squeezed through by very young Cavies and as the whole structure should stand on legs at least 2ft. high to prevent the inhabitants being frightened by Dogs or inundated with slush in inclement weather, it will be appreciated that they would risk some considerable nose dive to *terra firma*.

Should your Cavies be kept outside, and this appears to be the best method of keeping them, the top of their cage must be covered with roofing felt or some other waterproof material. Otherwise your stock runs grave risk of dying from pneumonia soon after the Spring or Autumn rains

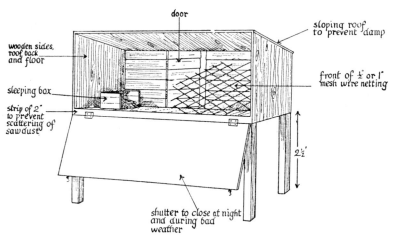

Fig. 1. Suitable hutch for Cavies.

start, and it is important, too, to site their home carefully, avoiding positions which face North or East or draughty corners. Entrance to the cage must be through a well-fitting door situated at one end or at the back, and should be of sufficient size to allow you to reach through in something like comfort when cleaning out.

In my opinion the sleeping compartment need not be an elaborate job of the type one so often sees provided for Rabbits. A sort of 'second room', in fact an ordinary small wooden box, minus its lid and placed on its side in the corner furthest from the door makes an admirable dormitory if half-filled with clean dry straw which, incidentally, is an ideal grooming agent for the Cavies' coats.

It is a good plan to paint the outside of the cage with a good wood preservative such as Cuprinol which is made in quite a range of colours, although green is perhaps the most attractive; the interior will look all the better for a coat of limewash, although this serves no really useful purpose other than of aesthetic merit and also, perhaps, to show up the inhabitants rather more clearly.

Although these animals are rodents they do not seem to gnaw the woodwork of their cages to the extent that Rats, Mice or Rabbits do, but it is nevertheless advisable to provide them with a piece of non-poisonous branch (almost any kind other than laburnum or conifers) on which they can exercise their perpetually growing teeth, and which will at the same time discourage them from chewing holes in their homes as is sometimes their wont.

The cage floor should have a reasonably thick covering of sawdust which should frequently be swept out and renewed; every day is advisable although no harm will be done if cleaning operations take place every other day, especially in the cold months of the year; but there is absolutely no excuse whatever for the individuals who clean their charges out once weekly and I am afraid these, mainly waster breeders, are surprisingly common.

So much for the conventional type of Cavy cage — perfectly good in its way and having stood the test of time, but how generally unimaginative.

Years ago one George Jennison, for a long time Director of the Manchester Zoological Gardens, said that the Cavy was an intelligent animal whose mental capacity was not properly appreciated and that its owner would get far more pleasure out of his pets if he gave them greater opportunities for their amusement. In other words they ought to be given something to do. As curator of a Zoological Gardens I heartily concur with this suggestion, as an intelligent creature which has nothing to do is often a most unhappy one, and no good livestock keeper wants his charges to be dull and morose; in fact it is not uncommon for captive animals to die years before their time from sheer boredom.

While experimenting along these lines as a boy, I walled

in a corner of the garden with some bricks which I obtained by demolishing an old decaying outbuilding. Inside the area I dug a shallow ravine, built miniature mounds of rock, made small cave-like recesses and, most important, a weatherproof sleeping shelter. In here I put one boar and, I think, three sow Cavies who immediately settled down amazingly well in their new and rather unusual abode. I never tired of watching the amusing way in which they would explore nooks and crannies or lie basking in the sun in a way I have never seen a caged specimen do. The shelter was situated on a small knoll

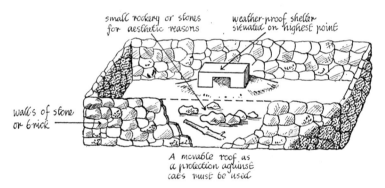

small rockery or stones for aesthetic reasons

weather-proof shelter situated on highest point

walls of stone or brick

A movable roof as a protection against cats must be used

Fig. 2. Suitable outdoor enclosure for Cavies.

so the rain or mud would not seep in during bad weather and the enclosure was sufficiently large not to become a mud wallow by the action of the inhabitants' feet at such times. On the whole the experiment was a great success, although I realize now that it was anything but Cat-proof; yet we were never troubled by these predators which seems rather a mystery as they were very plentiful locally – there were several of our own for example, but they had always been educated not to interfere with other animals. After nearly a year's service the enclosure was demolished to make room for an aviary and therefore the ground never really had time to become stale and sour, but, of course, this would have happened had it remained in use indefinitely and it would have had a most detrimental effect on the Cavies, which would have had to be removed while the ground was limed and allowed to lie fallow for some time.

Should the reader be thinking along these lines and contemplating building something similar he will find almost boundless scope for his imagination in this direction, but at the same time should bear in mind that it will not long remain the stretch of green sward it was before he introduced his stock, as in a short time they will have removed all edible greenstuff.

Of prime importance is the sound construction of the sleeping shelter as these animals are not quite as hardy as, say, Rabbits, and care must also be taken to see that it is placed sufficiently high up not to be buried by snow in winter – in fact all things considered I think it is advisable to keep Cavies in such an enclosure all the year round only in our Southern counties, where the snow is often hardly worth calling such. Cats, and Dogs, are likely to be a bugbear but can be thwarted by a movable wire-netting top stapled over a light wooden framework and rested neatly on the walls, whence it can easily be lifted when cleaning or feeding is in progress.

Yes, I can thoroughly recommend a colony of Cavies kept in such a place, but remember to limit the number of your boars or there may be some ripped ears caused through fighting.

On rather similar lines is the type of portable outdoor pen which many fanciers use during the warmer months of the year to enable their stock to get a little fresh air and grass. This structure resembles the rectangular wire pen in which, usually with coop attached, young chicks are kept in their early days. As the bottom is of wire-netting the inhabitants can easily feed on whatever type of herbage the run has been placed upon, and indeed might well be utilised as a form of living lawn mower if the position of their makeshift home be moved as and when they have finished at each particular place.

Needless to say the size of whatever type of cage you intend to use is going to depend on the number of animals you have, because almost as many as you wish can be kept 'under one roof'. The type of place, or any variations thereon, which I tried to describe at the beginning of this chapter is perfectly suitable, although, as I say, somewhat lacking in imagination; yet I have seen fine sturdy Cavies in perfect health kept under what one would have thought were bad conditions to say the least. Small wooden boxes scrounged from the grocer, fronted with wire-netting which one 'unhooked' from protruding nails along the top and down the sides, and situated in damp dingy sheds, have housed sound lively stock, while some of the best specimens I have ever seen were kept in aquarium tanks in a schoolroom; yet on the other hand I have not infrequently noticed professionally made cages containing scientifically kept specimens which were almost drooping.

Why this should be is by no means easy to explain, but some years ago I asked a doctor if he could suggest why it was that cleanly kept, decently fed animals often did not do as well or breed as freely as those kept under what might be termed slum conditions. He thought for a few minutes and then confessed that he was nonplussed, but added 'I know what you mean though, and have often noticed a more or less similar thing in Man. Sometimes some old recluse is found in a near derelict house, verminous, dirty and dressed in rags. He is brought into the hospital, given a bath, put between clean sheets and offered decent food – and as like as not he is dead at the end of a week'.

There is plenty of food for thought here, and doubtless nearly every fancier has noticed similar circumstances in stock he has seen elsewhere, but please do not think that I condone with such treatment: I heartily deplore it and merely offer it as a talking point for what it is worth. I suppose everyone thinks that if the Cavies he owns were not his they would probably not be as well kept, which is perhaps a healthy attitude to adopt as it shows a pride and affection for his charges, and in these materialistic days such a feeling is, I think, extremely valuable.

In conclusion, try to observe the behaviour of your charges and from it deduce the type of cage or alterations to it which suits them most, and on these lines you are not likely to go far wrong as far as housing is concerned.

CHAPTER THREE

Feeding

THE FEEDING of the domestic Cavy is a simple matter if one bears in mind that by nature it is a vegetarian, like a Rabbit, and in fact can be fed in exactly the same way as the latter animal.

I am afraid that in this age and day certain mercenary individuals condemn their Rabbits to a diet consisting almost entirely of highly concentrated pellets so that they will grow faster and heavier than would be normal, in order to make fatter profits on them. The Rabbit which is fed in the way it was meant to feed is getting somewhat rare, but so far this commercialized 'animal factorying' has not touched the Cavy, and I devoutly hope never will.

Primarily your Cavies' food should consist of good fresh greenstuff which during the Spring and Summer can almost be collected entirely from the neighbouring lane-sides and fields where will be found nearly infinite variety – dandelion, groundsel (not too much of this, however), shepherds' purse, cow parsley, sow thistle, clover, chickweed, plantains, vetch and many others, not forgetting, of course, the many varieties of grasses. These latter, however, do not appear to be very sustaining in themselves and whenever our Cavies have a meal consisting solely of grass it is only a short time before it has all disappeared and they are clamouring and 'winking' for more.

Needless to add, many common native plants are to a greater or lesser extent poisonous and must be avoided at

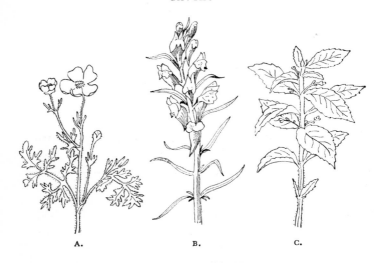

FIG. 3. SOME POISONOUS PLANTS

A. Buttercup   D. Ragwort
B. Toadflax   E. Foxglove
C. Dog's Mercury   F. Hemlock

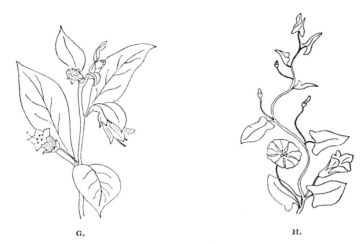

G.   H.

FIG. 4.   MORE POISONOUS PLANTS
G. Deadly Nightshade   H. Convolvulus

all costs, although, unfortunately, there does not appear
to be a comprehensive and illustrated list of them available to the lay public. Among the commoner ones, though,
may be mentioned bindweed, foxglove, yew (deadly – and
deceptive; many animals eat it greedily), laburnum,
buttercup, bryony, anemone, nightshade, privet and
travellers' joy. On the whole it often appears that damp,
low lying, shady places are far more likely to nourish
poisonous plants than sunny upland spots, so this may
serve as a very rough guide, although you must beware of
placing too much reliance on it. If, when gathering
fodder, you come upon a plant you are not certain about,
leave it severely alone.

Apart from the more conventional foodstuffs such as
carrots, turnips, cabbage, lettuce and kale from the
garden, you could also safely feed marigolds (a great
blessing if they are getting too plentiful), bramble cuttings

and the prunings from elm and ash trees, although these extras can hardly be classed as major food items.

During the Winter, feeding is not quite such an easy matter owing to the dearth of greenstuff available. It is then that the Cavy fancier has to rely largely on such items as hay, roots, bread and such brassicas as cabbage and kale as and when they are available, although, of course, he does not have quite such a difficult time if he happens to have a farmer among his friends. A good standby is a mixture of clean kitchen waste, consisting largely of vegetable peelings, which is boiled until soft and then mixed thoroughly with a slightly smaller quantity of bran; but avoid mixing this valuable food with sodden tea-leaves alone – as so many people do – as the latter commodity contains no food value worth talking about. Incidentally, it is distinctly dangerous to offer dry bran alone as it usually creates some considerable thirst, and water preceded by bran can be fatal.

Although rather expensive, fruit is usually obtainable throughout the Winter and an allowance of the proverbial 'apple a day' per specimen will ensure that it will receive at least some vitamin C all the year round, as this is found only in fruit and vegetables and the body cannot store it, so a supply must always be offered. Vitamin C deficiency can cause some decidedly unpleasant things – dull staring coats are about the least damaging of its products. In the old windjammer days it was the direct cause of the dreaded scurvy among the crews.

At our Zoo we keep several domestic Goats to supply many of the denizens of the gardens with milk and what is known as Coarse Dairy Mixture. The latter, ostensibly for adding to their diet to boost milk production, frequently finds its way into the food dishes of the various small rodents. This, we feel is excellent for them as not only is it very rich in protein (which promotes rapid and sound natural growth in young stock) but contains such items as dairy nuts, linseed oil cake and locust bean which are 'just right' for exercising the strong chisel-like teeth of these animals; the Cavies in particular seem to enjoy it and the youngsters put on flesh in a hitherto unknown way.

One question I am often asked is, 'How much food should a Cavy be given daily?'. This is extremely difficult to answer as no two animals have identical appetites and in any case they all have their 'off days' from time to time when less than normal is eaten, while on the other hand it is not uncommon for one individual occasionally to eat far more than he usually does, for no apparent reason. Whether you keep one or a dozen Cavies give two feeds daily, morning and evening – and notice how much is eaten: if the whole lot is devoured in a short time and the diners stand around in a vague and hopeful fashion you can rest assured that you are not being over-generous a caterer, but if a fair quantity is left to be wasted and trodden into the sawdust you are being rather extravagant and should regulate future feeds accordingly. It is simply a matter of trial and error, but in a few days you should begin to understand the individual tastes of each animal and interpret a conversational 'wink' and one which clearly says, 'What time do we eat round here?'.

'To give water or not to give water, that is the question', and a very old one too, as fanciers have for long debated the advisability of giving water to Cavies; some declared that it is essential to their general well-being while others maintained that if plenty of fresh greenstuff were present in the diet such 'coddling' was unnecessary. Some Cavies never see a drop of water and look none the worse for it, even going on to win at shows, but we give ours fresh water daily and their reactions to it are rather interesting. On the whole they do not regard it as a particularly popular beverage and take but little of it, especially when there is an abundance of natural herbage available, but during hot weather they drink freely and the pots may have to be replenished more than once during the day; again, they will sometimes take it avidly during quite cool periods after ignoring it for some time, which seems to us quite inexplicable. Briefly summing up the water situation I would say that these animals are not great drinkers but must always have water available (in a squat shaped vessel they cannot easily knock over) just in case.

Never make the mistake of feeding a Cavy (or any other animal) on too dry a diet or he may become a prolapsed rectum case (more of this later), while it is nearly equally important to avoid offering nothing but greenstuff, or diarrhoea may result. One has to strike the happy medium in the way of a sensible and balanced diet. It must continually be borne in mind that other animals differ individually just as much as we do and that it will pay dividends for the enthusiastic fancier to study each of his charges and become *au fait* with particular fads and characteristics – a knowledge of what one particular animal regards as a *bonne bouche* may one day save its life if it falls ill and has to be given some cunningly disguised medicine.

The greatest Cavy personality it was ever my pleasure to know was one of the first I ever owned, a boar of no particular variety and rejoicing in the name of Roger, which I think was bestowed on him by my small sister. Although officially mine, he was her special pet and, incredible as it may sound, would allow her to take him for walks on a collar and lead, while on more than one occasion I found her cuddling a queer little figure in human dress, which looked from a distance like some hirsute satyr but turned out to be Roger clad in doll's clothes. Needless to say I soon put a stop to this as I consider the dressing up of animals undignified to say the very least, but I suspect that it still went on when I was at school. It was in his peculiar choice of titbits, however, that this curious Cavy excelled, for of all things he liked trifle. It appears that one day his custodian was eating one of the horribly gaudy sixpenny trifles that were obtainable at that time and seeing him watching her in an interested way offered him a little in the spoon; this was eagerly lapped up and another helping searched for, which was really the start of the craze, as for a long time after he had his regularly sixpenny concoction of sodden sponge cake, viscous custard and artificial cream. Roger's end came suddenly and regrettably; it was Guy Fawke's Night, 1945, and he was in the act of eating his evening feed – it was boiled potatoes, I remember – when there came a veritable cacophany of firework detonations from the garden next door, just a yard or so from his cage; some were thrown over to explode a matter of inches from him and the result was that he died from what I now realize was heart failure. Since then I must have owned literally hundreds of Cavies but have yet to come upon one with anything approaching the personality of the most remarkable one I have ever known.

We appear to have deviated somewhat from the main theme of this chapter, so it might be a good plan to conclude it with a very businesslike list of DOS and DO NOTS which I hope may prove of use to the novice:

DO give your Cavies a varied diet; how would you like to live entirely on duck and green peas?

DO make sure, that they have clean water constantly available.

DO learn to distinguish poisonous plants if you are not already familiar with them.

DO remember to give your stock some form of fresh fruit or vegetable throughout the year.

DO NOT offer herbage which might have been fouled by Cats or Dogs.

DO NOT feed your stock by throwing food onto a dirty cage floor; this is just asking for trouble.

DO NOT give dry bran, or bran mixed with tea leaves.

DO NOT suddenly switch young newly purchased stock over to a new diet they are not familiar with, or internal disorders may result. Ascertain what they have been used to at the time of buying, and make any subsequent changes gradually.

DO NOT give large quantities of lettuce – this contains laudanum, and can be fed safely only in small helpings.

DO NOT offer much white bread which contains a harmful chemical known as agene; brown bread is much better.

DO NOT give lawn mowings which have been heaped up for some time until they have begun to ferment.

DO NOT forget to add a little cod liver oil to your stock's food during the winter as the vitamin D it contains makes up for the sunshine they are missing. This applies particularly to those which are kept indoors.

CHAPTER FOUR

Breeding

THERE EXISTS a widespread and erroneous belief that Cavies breed at a rate more normally associated with Rabbits or Mice, which is rather difficult to comprehend as they are in fact, for small domestic mammals, very slow reproducers indeed. Often reluctant to mate (I have known it take a pair over three months before they decided to consummate the marriage I arranged for them), their litters are very small (three youngsters is about the average) and the gestation period long, while abortions and stillbirths are surprisingly common – all of which makes the popular myth even more of a mystery.

Actually Cavy breeding is very easy indeed as the young are precocious from birth and therefore do not run the risk of being eaten by some over nervous mother as they would if they were blind and helpless like, say, the Rabbit. They are born with a full complement of hair, their eyes are open and their milk teeth already shed; they can walk at the age of one hour and start experimentally nibbling solid food a day later. As a rule they are suckled for only a matter of three weeks or so and very soon after they are ignored by their dams, who are perhaps pregnant again as these animals sometimes copulate again the day their young are produced, which is perhaps the only grain of truth in the legend of their promiscuousness: but then so do Horses and Cats. . .

It is perfectly safe to leave a boar and sow Cavy together in the cage while you are hoping for them to mate, as there will be no risk of the latter attacking and injuring the former as would be likely to happen in the Rabbit, but one can never be certain that mating has actually taken place as these animals seem very secretive about this and on only one occasion in all the years I have kept them have I observed the act of copulation. The gestation period is quite long, sixty-three to seventy-five days in fact, although usually it is in the neighbourhood of the first figure, and if you regard it as being roughly that of a Dog you will not be far out. In many mammals the uterus (the hollow muscular organ in which the unborn young are carried) is situated rather high up in the body and consequently there is little external sign of the condition of a pregnant female, but in the Cavy this is not so and the impending family is much in evidence long before it is born. During the latter weeks of pregnancy it is advisable to handle the sow as little as possible as it is likely that excessive handling is the cause of many cases of still-born young. At the same time her daily diet should be considerably increased or puny youngsters which she may not be able to feed properly could result.

It is not necessary to segregate the gravid sow before the birth irrespective of whether she is housed with only a single boar or kept in a colony of any size. In the latter case there is not likely to be any interference with the young from other sows as these animals are naturally gregarious and in a state of domestication show a marked preference for the communal mode of life.

It is perhaps best to remove Cavies which you wish to dispose of from their mothers at the age of about four or five weeks when they will be quite capable of looking after themselves. At this juncture it is important not to change them over to a diet they have not been used to or severe internal troubles may result, and it is as well to remember that the domestic Cavy is one of the most difficult of all animals to treat when ill. If you keep pedigree animals you should have little difficulty in selling them if you offer them for sale in *Fur and Feather*, which seems to be the only weekly publication in which they are dealt with in anything like detail. It is read by fanciers all over the country and the advertisement columns are eagerly scanned by those who wish to add new blood to their studs. 'Wasters' or those which are not pure bred are not quite so easy to sell, although many pet shops are willing to offer a few shillings each for them, which may suit you perfectly. It might also be a good plan to offer such animals in the 'Pets' columns of the local papers – I suspect the results might be quite encouraging. If you find it impossible to dispose of your wasters it would be best to segregate the sexes of your adults or at least control your matings carefully before you have a larger number of Cavies than you can conveniently care for, house or feed.

One word of warning: one frequently sees advertisements asking for ordinary wasters in quantity but stipulating that they must be of a certain weight, usually about 16oz. My advice is not to send yours to such a place as it may be some laboratory wanting to experiment on them. I know that in making this plea I sound like some middle-aged female crank, but I am not. I am a zoologist, curator of a Zoological Gardens, male and aged twenty-seven – but I know something of what is involved.

We will say that you live in the Midlands and that someone from Scotland has bought some of your stock; what is the best way of despatching it? First, find out the time of the best train to wherever it is, together with the (anticipated) time of arrival and notify your buyer, so that if the animals do not arrive at the specified time (which I am afraid is rather likely, unless it is a through train) he can assume that something is amiss and start

B

making enquiries from his end. Pack the Cavies in a strong wooden box with a generous layer of clean new hay on the bottom and provide them with some 'sandwiches' for the journey – carrots are ideal for this purpose as their very juiciness makes them an excellent thirst-quencher – and, needless to add, ensure that there is adequate ventilation. Do not forget to head the address label with a bold LIVESTOCK and also add your own name and address, just in case something goes wrong en route. It is well worth paying the little extra to send any form of livestock at Company's risk, rather than the owner's.

It is a simple matter to determine the sex of your Cavies, even at the early age of one day and as I heartily agree with the Chinese that one picture is worth a thousand words of explanation, propose to do no more than offer the following diagrams:

Fig. 5.

Male   Female

According to some life-long fanciers, sow Cavies never kill and eat their young as happens in so many other species, which, for all I know, may be perfectly true; but it seems an almost invariable, or at least very common, rule that those which are still-born or which die at an early age are partially or wholly devoured.

Cavies mate far more readily during the warmer months of the year, say between April and September, than in the cold damp ones of Autumn and Winter, but the judicious addition of a little wheat germ oil to their food over this latter period may well induce them to breed although care will have to be taken to ensure that the young are well protected from the weather. Wheat germ oil is almost straight vitamin E which induces fertility, and can be purchased from practically any chemist although it is fairly expensive; a supply would, however, be a very wise investment as in the past I have found it extremely efficacious with several types of livestock which were either reluctant or unable to breed.

As I mentioned earlier, Cavies usually give birth to very small litters – those of two or three being the most common, although I have known of several which consisted of a single youngster only, and one case of quins, but this number appears to be of very rare occurrence. The record for a Cavy litter is always given as ten, but no other details about this phenomenon seem to be available, or, indeed, known.

Sometimes a sow will give birth to a litter which she will refuse to have anything to do with until either they die or you take over the hand rearing of them; this is most common in young animals and, as far as I can see, is nature's way of preparing the female's system for the reception of future litters – in other words the first young were never meant to survive, but were almost gynaeco-logical practice! Of course, this is by no means invariably the case and every breeder of animals could speak of excellent specimens he has bred from 'first time' mothers, but it is surprising how many first litters are puny, half-heartedly looked after, or ignored altogether, especially in wild animals. Incidentally, it is a good plan not to handle your young stock more frequently than is necessary, as in my experience excessive handling is rather inclined to stunt a young animal's growth.

There is, by the way, a very widespread notion among breeders of many kinds of domestic animals that it is the male of the species which is responsible for the number of young in a litter. This is completely erroneous, as all he has to do is fertilize the ova of the female, who is, in fact, the one responsible for the number of young.

CHAPTER FIVE

Showing

To SHOW OR NOT TO SHOW, that is the question – and quite a big one too, as there are many fanciers whose interest in Cavies centres primarily around this activity and would declare the hobby a somewhat pointless one were it not for the culmination of their breeding experiments in this form. In all fairness I think I had better admit here and now that I have no interest in showing whatsoever, whether the subjects be Cavies or chrysanthemums – much to the disgust of my wife who finds great pleasure in exhibiting her beloved Old English Sheepdogs. It appears that showing is a matter about which one has strong views, irrespective of the light in which it is seen – one either considers it a jolly fine pursuit with no betters and few equals, or just the reverse! Mediocre opinions are extremely rare. Personally I find the whole attitude of mind behind showing – that of 'Look what I've got, boys, it's better than yours' – somewhat infantile and a little distasteful, but as the beginner wants to know how to set about showing his stock and not what my views are on the matter let us look along the path he will have to take.

Cavies which are not pure bred are not eligible for showing, and pure bred stock which is mismarked (*see chapter on varieties*) stands little, if any, chance of winning, although it may be entered for competition. Sickly specimens should never be sent to a show, no matter how good they may be otherwise, as their chances of success are remote, apart from the fact that they may well spread whatever they may be sickening for among their fellow competitors.

If you decide to 'go in for showing' I suggest that you place an order with your newsagent for a copy of *Fur and Feather* each week (every Thursday to be precise) which will contain whole pages devoted entirely to listing shows of the type where Cavies are catered for. During the Summer it is a good plan to keep an eye open for posters advertising agricultural and county shows, which often put on classes for these animals. The next step is to write to the show secretary, whose name invariably appears at the foot of the notice, and ask for a schedule to be sent to you. When this arrives study it carefully and decide which classes you wish to enter your particular Cavies in, or perhaps it might be more correct to say which classes you *can* enter them in, as these are very carefully planned. Usually any one class caters only for one specific variety and none other, especially where the commoner types are concerned, although there are quite often special classes for the less popular colours which would not be numerous enough to merit a class to themselves, and in these cases all comers compete irrespective of their 'race'. When you have selected the classes in which you propose entering your most promising specimens, fill in the form attached to the schedule without delay (there is always a dead-line after which entries will not be accepted, which is perfectly understandable) and send it to the secretary, without forgetting to enclose the necessary postal order or cheque to cover the cost of your classes. The fee charged is extremely reasonable when one considers the high cost of running such an event, with such headaches as the hiring of the room, hall or marquee, the hiring of the benches and pens, the printing of the catalogues and the amount of secretarial work which precedes it all.

Many fanciers, in fact I think it might almost be safe to say the majority of them, do not, as a rule, attend the shows at which they exhibit their stock but prefer to send it on by rail, perfectly happy in the knowledge that it will be promptly met at the other end and generally given every care and attention until it is returned to them after the show. It is because of this that each exhibitor receives, a few days before the event, a special 'livestock, with care' label to attach to the Cavies' travelling box if he wishes to send them in this way.

I think at this juncture a few words on the pros and cons of taking stock to a show oneself would not be out of place, as the decision depends entirely upon the type of show concerned. If I were exhibiting (if!) I would accompany my stock to a county or agricultural show, but send it on its own to one devoted entirely to Rabbits, Cavies and the like. The reason is not far to seek, and I am afraid it is rather a selfish one. Both types of show usually last from somewhere in the neighbourhood of ten-thirty in the morning to about five-thirty in the evening, and whereas at the latter type one spends, after having inspected all the other stock, several dreary hours in some gloomy school or drill hall (both of which places might well revive unpleasant memories) eagerly waiting for the time when one is permitted to remove one's stock and scamper home, at the former class of show things are rather more attractive. Here, after the exhibitor has seen the results of the judging, he can walk out into the sunshine (or otherwise) and inspect the other attractions which will be many and varied; the immense wealth of plant life in the flower marquees, the classes for Cattle, Pigs, Horses and Dogs, others for aquaria, cage birds and home produce, and perhaps some of the more unusual ones such as thatching competitions or the shoeing of huge and patient Shire horses. Under such conditions the time may well pass all too quickly – and may the day be made all the more pleasant by the knowledge that your Cavies have done well on their particular show bench.

Incidentally I should mention that if the exhibitor lives a certain distance, or over, from the actual venue of the show, he receives what is known as an early removal pass so that, if he attends himself, he can leave, together with his stock, some time before the show would normally end – a great blessing for those who have a long journey to make, possibly in pelting rain on a windy Autumn night.

When Cavies are sent to shows by rail it is the normal procedure to despatch them in a special travelling box which is usually divided up into sections; these are often offered for sale, either new or second-hand in the previously mentioned magazine, but the handyman may prefer to make his own, which I am rather in favour of. Make sure that each section or compartment has a generous bed of hay which will serve as a shock absorber during the possibly lengthy train journey. Almost needless to add, ensure that the case is despatched in good time as it will be infuriating to learn that your entries arrived on the first train after the show had begun and, no one knowing they were there, had to wait many hours on the station until the stewards, sending other and more punctual entries back to their homes, discovered them when the show was over.

Fanciers who prefer to take their stock to shows will not be concerned with the possibility of this sort of thing occurring, which, as often as not, may be the fault of the railway company, and not dilatoriness on the part of the exhibitor.

On arrival at the venue one must hand one's entries over to a steward who attaches to their ears a series of gummed paper labels, each of which bears the number of the pen which that particular specimen will occupy for the duration of its stay at the show. He then installs them in the said pens where they have a chance of settling down after the journey and thus be steady and unruffled when later handled by the judge. This latter point is really very important as a judge will sometimes refuse to consider a Cavy which, through being generally upset and unsettled, squirms actively when handled and refuses to allow itself to be examined. Some frequently-shown specimens, by the way, become such old hands at the game that they seem to know just what is expected of them and practically 'play the part' of being good exhibits; one can almost see them nodding patronizingly towards their beaming owners and saying 'Oh well, it's amusing them and it's not hurting us'.

When the actual judging starts the judge will occupy a centrally placed table with stewards stationed on either side to bring exhibits from their pens and return them as and when required. Incidentally it is interesting to note that, in theory, only a steward can handle any Cavy during a show; just how rigidly this is adhered to I really don't know, but it is what the book of rules specifically states; of course, it does not apply to the judge who has to handle the exhibits in order to assess which he considers the best.

Of the actual judging I have but little to say as the whole thing is all so arbitrary. By this I mean that a Cavy with a deeper coloured coat than its neighbour is regarded as being a 'better' one, or another is condemned as being 'bad' because its head is not as broad as it might be or its ears are not quite the 'right' shape – all of which strikes me as being singularly ridiculous.

The Cavy which comes top in its class is given a red card or certificate, the second a blue one, and the third and fourth yellow and green ones respectively, while those which do not quite make the grade but are regarded as being highly commended receive white tokens.

At these shows the newcomer can learn an enormous amount of Cavy lore by introducing himself to the many fanciers of long experience who will be there in force, and by frankly asking their advice on any points which may be worrying or puzzling him in any aspect of the hobby. Almost invariably he will be willingly given a wealth of advice and, no doubt, many invitations to visit their homes and see their own studs for himself. Visits of this nature are usually well worth while as no two fanciers have the same methods, whether it be feeding, housing, breeding or treatment during sickness, and many useful hints and tips are certain to be picked up in this way. At the same time do not hesitate to return their hospitality as, who knows, you may well have some perfectly good ideas of your own which the others might never have thought of – thus do fanciers constantly strive to improve the lot of their stock, as do all good animal keepers.

Earlier I mentioned that a Cavy which has been entered for a show must be in perfect condition, which applies not only in the bodily sense but also regarding the state of its coat and its general deportment and demeanour. A specimen which is rather listless and sluggish, although otherwise in apparently perfect health, stands little chance on the show-bench in competition with others which have that little extra 'bloom' about them.

Before sending a Cavy to a show one should treat it to a thorough though light grooming with a reasonably stiff brush (a child's hair brush is ideal) which will not only beautify the coat but also remove any dead or loose hairs which may be present. Also make sure that there are no overgrown toenails (*vide chapter on ailments*) which would certainly reduce his chances on 'the field of battle'. If you are among the comparative minority of people who keep either Peruvian or Abyssinian Cavies you will, naturally, have to pay much more attention to grooming than is the case among the smooth-haired fanciers. These two types are dealt with in greater detail elsewhere in this book, but suffice it to say at the moment that Peruvians have almost incredibly long hair and Abyssinians a shorter and more wiry pelage which is arranged in a most intricate pattern of rosettes. It is not the slightest use grooming these types only before shows, as if neglected, even for only a comparatively short time, they will become an unattractive mass of clots and tangles, especially in the case of the Peruvians. In this variety the hair should be gently combed at least once a week, and any tangles found, carefully 'unpicked' by hand, although these should be *non est* in a well cared for specimen. Many Peruvian fanciers bath their stock before shows, and to a non-aquatic creature like the domestic Cavy this smacks slightly of cruelty to me, although I suppose the more seasoned exhibits get used to this procedure in time. After the tubbing the hair has to be put into brown paper curlers lest it curl – which a good Peruvian's should *never* do!

While the Abyssinian's coat is less likely to become tangled it must have frequent attention paid to its rosettes and mane, the latter being a scruff of coarse hair at the back of the head, which continues in the form of a ridge through to the rump.

In brief it may be mentioned that Cavy showing can be an absorbing hobby for those who enjoy competitive exhibiting, and, admittedly, it does encourage one to keep one's stock in tip-top form at all times, but the novice must not be discouraged if at first he fails to do well on the show-bench. All the most successful fanciers have had their earlier periods of disappointment and frustration when they felt that their stock would never make the grade, but there is nothing like tenacity of purpose to carry one through trying times. If the beginner is really determined to breed winning stock one day the chances are heavily in favour of the ultimate realization of his aim.

CHAPTER SIX

Varieties of Cavies

As I mentioned in an earlier chapter, the development of the Cavy as a domestic animal is very largely shrouded in mystery – metaphorically speaking it was here as a wild animal one minute and present in a multitude of varieties and forms the next; what happened in between is largely anybody's guess. This is made all the more surprising by the fact that there are so many distinct varieties of these animals which apparently sprang from nowhere in such a comparatively short time. Although there are probably quite a number yet to be bred and shown for the first time these will be rather less intriguing as their development will be closely observed – as has happened with not a few of the more recent of the extant types.

Basically, Cavies are present in three distinct forms: smooth-haired, Peruvian and Abyssinian, although their differences are only those of coat texture – beneath they are all honest-to-goodness *Cavia porcella*. The first group are what might well be termed the common or conventional Cavies as they possess the short smooth coat which clothes the vast majority of those offered for sale in pet stores or similar places, or, on more aristocratic specimens, at divers shows up and down the country; I think it would be safe to say that seven out of ten Cavies belong to this group. Next come the Peruvians with their exaggeratedly long coats which completely mask their physical features to such an extent that some exceptional specimens resemble no known animal; and finally there are the

Abyssinians which have an even pattern of intricate rosettes practically covering their bodies, which are surmounted by crests of fur running along the spine. Despite the peculiarities of the last two types they can be bred in most of the very wide range of colours in which the smooth haired appear and, of course, being, zoologically speaking, the same animal, will readily breed with them. This would, of course, be frowned on by the serious breeder who wishes to preserve the purity of his stock.

Each variety of Cavy has its own particular characteristics which distinguish it from all others, and it is the development of these mainly physical features of colour or markings in the individual which determine whether or not it is a good or poor show specimen. Every variety has a table of points, or, to give it its proper title, a standard, setting down just what the ideal specimen should look like, together with a list of faults which no show Cavy should possess; but it must be borne in mind that these virtues are largely arbitrary and have little or no bearing on whether the Cavy concerned is robust and sound organically, which is what really matters in my opinion.

All domestic Cavies fall into one of two classes, Self or Marked, the latter so called because they have two or more colours, one of which usually forms some definite 'pattern' or marking on the body, while the former are of one, and only one, colour throughout. Let us deal with this group first.

Whatever the colour of a Self Cavy, it should be deep, clear and rich – in fact such great emphasis is placed on colour on the show-bench that perfection in this direction can win a higher number of points for a Cavy than any of its other attributes; thirty out of a possible hundred in fact. Next in order of merit comes its general conformation with no less than twenty-five points – officially this states that a good Cavy should have a short cobby body, deep broad shoulders and a Roman nose; this all seems a little vague to me as I should say that virtually all the specimens I have seen have looked just like this. Next in order of importance comes the coat which must be short, smooth, and fairly glossy and for which fifteen points are awarded. According to the standard the ears must be rose shaped, whatever that might mean, spaced widely apart, and should droop slightly, although it must be remembered that this portion of the Cavy's anatomy is very often most irregularly shaped owing to the fact that the edges are frequently attacked by some strange though mild encrustations (probably fungoid) which destroy the tissues, although the general health of the 'sufferer' is usually in no way impaired.

The eyes should be large, clear and bold and, like the ears, will earn their owner another ten points, as also does good condition. This latter point is rather surprising as it clearly implies that in the opinion of the Cavy Fancy good health and condition is no more highly regarded than the unimportant shape of the ear or the size of the eye; actually sound health is a vital factor and one might have expected it to have been awarded a much higher place on the list of points.

This, then, gives a rough idea of the general physical conformation of a Self Cavy of show standard, the only way in which the various varieties differ from each other being that of colour. There are at the present day about seven colour forms available to the fancier, although some are far more popular and easily obtained than others, so let us look at them.

WHITE. This is one of the most familiar and popular of all the Cavies, its coat being pure white, its ears a delicate pink and the eyes apparently red. In other words it is, of course, an albino and as such is colourless through lack of pigmentation in the system, the eyes being quite transparent and giving the illusion of redness only because the blood vessels in and at the back of them are clearly visible. Few things in the animal kingdom look worse than a dirty White Cavy which is really very easy to maintain in immaculate coat if provided with an abundance of fresh straw or hay for bedding, into which it can tunnel and burrow to its heart's content, and at the same time keep its coat spotlessly clean.

Some time ago there appeared in the United States an outsize strain known, rather dramatically, as the Giant White Cavy. Just what size this Leviathan attains is by no means clear as very little indeed seems to be known about it in this country, but it is interesting to note that the White Cavy has always tended to grow to a rather larger size than the other types, with the result that it frequently becomes rather coarse and has to be crossed with smaller stock in order to regain lost quality; therefore it would appear that producing a 'giant' type of this variety would not be a difficult matter. There also exists a White Cavy with black eyes instead of the normal 'red' but these are generally regarded by experienced fanciers as being of a much poorer type than the standard strain; they are certainly very much rarer.

BLACK. When in tip top condition this lovely variety has a glossy coat which almost shimmers and looks literally like satin, yet, rather surprisingly, really good blacks are by no means common as a great many have a scattering of hairs of a different colour – mainly white, although red ones sometimes crop up. These unwanted hairs are not necessarily permanencies however, as at the time of writing we have a Black sow which was presented to us by a rather disgruntled owner who found some white hairs on the head and neck of this otherwise perfect show

(*above*) Mounted specimen of the 'mystery' Cavy, possible ancestor of the domestic Cavy, in the Manchester Museum

The Author's son, Jeremy shows how to handle a Cavy

3. A family of Cavies bred on the colony system; the youngsters seen here are only one day old

4. Tortoiseshell-and-White Cavy

5. Self-blacks, the property of Miss Weiston of Burton Joyce

6. Mr. J. Amott's Dutch Cavy—note the ear tag with the animal's show number

7. Young pink-eyed White Cavy

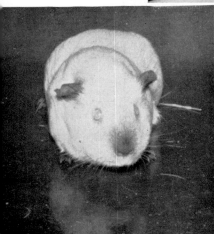

8. Himalayan Cavy, the property of Mr. Holmes of Beeston

9. Mr. Badcock judging Cavies at Nottingham

10. Two Abyssinians belonging to Mr. Kettle of Grimston

11. Mr. Bert Ellson with his Peruvian Cavy, Ch. Diana of Elton

Photo: Thompson Allied Newspapers

specimen. She was given quarters in the section devoted to domestic animals here and soon settled down; some months after her arrival she was visited by her late owner who expressed amazement on observing that the white blemishes had completely disappeared, as indeed they had, which was all rather surprising. Some Blacks look of a far less intense shade when compared with the others due to the fact that the undercoat is of a greyish or slatey tint which is quite a bad fault on the show-bench, and one which needs to be corrected, should it be present in one's stud, by means of judicious crossing with animals which are of a good deep black right down to the skin. Not only should the fur of this handsome animal be black, but also the ears and feet.

RED. Although there are many Cavies of many shades of red, the Fancy officially recognizes only those which are of a deep, almost mahogany, tint which must continue in its intensity right down to the skin with no paling below the surface. Individual specimens of this variety vary to a surprising extent – some even appearing in an almost orange shade while others are a definite saffron, but are nevertheless all classed as Reds. In good specimens the ears are of the same colour as the body, those which are dark being regarded as blemishes.

BEIGE. Good Cavies of this rather indeterminate colour should have a strong strain of fawn predominating, but not yellow on any account as this is classed as a fault. They have 'red' eyes, which suggest they are of some albino origin, and this should not really be difficult to trace by anyone who is interested as they are a comparatively recent strain whose family tree ought to be easy to track down.

LILAC. Just as a normal spotted Leopard might well give birth to a litter containing both normal and black (melanistic) cubs, so did many of the early Beige Cavies have both replicas of themselves and also another hitherto unknown colour in their litters. This latter was cultivated and now, known as the Lilac, breeds true to type and has many adherents in the Fancy. I always think that a little wishful thinking helped to give it its name as it bears little if any resemblance to the flower it is likened to (to be really technical the White Cavy might stake a more justified claim to bear this name as lilac blossoms of this shade are known to all!), and is in fact a quite pleasing dove-grey with, in some individual specimens, a slight pinkish tinge.

We are still reminded of their ancestry by the many specimens which appear with a definite Beige influence, but these are regarded as poor individuals for breeding with and are gradually being bred out although 'throwbacks' from the original stock occur from time to time in all forms of domestic animals, no matter how old a race they may belong to.

Although attractive, the Lilac Cavy is by no means common, and the enthusiast who wishes to make a start with them may well find some difficulty in obtaining his initial stock, which will probably be rather expensive. In the opinion of some people these Cavies are rather spoiled by their 'red' eyes, but to the serious breeder this is an interesting characteristic indicating their albino origin.

CREAM. This is a rather difficult colour to define as quite a number of breeders have their own ideas on the matter and produce strains of Creams which look rather dissimilar to each other. Officially, though, these animals should be of a pale and even cream which is totally free from any hint of yellow, a colour which tinges and spoils many specimens which are otherwise perfect. Another Cream to avoid is one which has an admixture of White blood as it may well have very pale underparts; yet many experienced fanciers deliberately cross their Cream stock in this way in order to produce a really pale type which they hope will do well on the show-bench.

CHOCOLATE. This very old established variety is today quite a rarity and I have not seen any offered for sale for some years now, which is a pity as they are lovely little creatures. Here again is a type which is inclined to vary in colour from stud to stud, despite the fact that the official description of one stresses the deep richness of its chocolate-coloured pelage. In all races of animals which are numerically small there is the very real danger of their becoming debilitated through inter-breeding, and to some extent this is what has happened, and is happening, with the Chocolate Cavy, which has nevertheless been crossed with the Black in order to give depth of colour where it has been needed. In such instances the new blood has done much to improve matters where general condition has been concerned.

So much for the Self Cavies; now to look at the marked varieties, one of the most attractive of which is the HIMALAYAN, which, rather surprisingly, is marked in just the same way as the Siamese Cat, except for the tail, of course! The body is, or should be, pure white, although in many rather inferior specimens it is often more of an ivory tint which is by no means as attractive; the nose, ears and feet are a deep sepia or seal brown and, yet again, the 'red' eyes reveal the albino ancestry. The Himalayan Rabbit, too, is coloured and marked in exactly the same way and for the fancier interested in genetics there is a wealth of study and exploration in probing into the origin of these three strangely marked animals, or more particularly, into just what produces the pigmentation in the extremities so shaded. That they are semi-albinos is obvious, but other than that we know really very little. The name Himalayan is a complete misnomer, as neither the Cavy or Rabbit concerned are in any remote way connected with those mountains; if they *had* to be given a fancy name surely it would have been more in keeping to have called them the Siamese, like the Cat which already bore that title.

I well remember reading an indignant letter in the correspondence column of a livestock periodical in which the writer complained that he had paid a good price for a sow Himalayan Cavy which was in pig (pregnant) and had been surprised and disappointed to find that when the youngsters arrived they were pure white and bore little resemblance to the mother; clearly he thought she had been mated to a White and he had been, in plain language, swindled. An editorial note, however, pointed out that all baby Himalayans look like this for the first two or three weeks of their lives and then start to 'brown over' on the salient points which slowly intensify in colour until the animal reaches maturity at the age of about six months. This, incidentally, proves even further their albino lineage.

In the Cat world the Siamese appears not only in the familiar 'seal' markings but also in 'blue' (slatey grey, really), red (usually known as 'ginger' to non-Cat breeders), tabby, chocolate, lilac and several other lesser known colours, and I am faintly surprised that Cavies and Rabbits have so far not appeared in any of them – surely there is a great deal of scope here for the enthusiast who might care to cross his Himalayans with, say, Lilacs or Reds, and not be discouraged by possible failures at first.

The density, or otherwise, of the seal points varies a

great deal from individual to individual and it is not uncommon to find odd specimens with such pale and 'washed out' feet, ears and noses that from a little distance they look for all the world like Whites. Great stress is laid on these markings in the official standard of points which makes quite interesting reading; thus no less than twenty points out of a total of a hundred are awarded for sheer density of the colour of the extremities, while a further fifteen are reserved for those noses so profusely shaded that they appear to extend almost up to the eyes. A pure white body earns another fifteen points, while ears which are shaded right down to their bases and feet which are similarly hued up to the legs are characteristics which merit another ten each; the same number is awarded for large eyes, a compact body and, last of all, of course, general condition.

In short the Himalayan Cavy is a truly beautiful and rather singular looking animal which is deservedly popular although it is not particularly easy to obtain, and would-be breeders are advised to scan the Cavies' 'For Sale' columns as soon as possible each week, as available stock is always snapped up very quickly.

I think there is little doubt that the most popular of the marked varieties is the DUTCH, which, like the foregoing, has its counterpart in the Rabbit world. Briefly it can be described as being white with the whole hindquarters very sharply divided off in some totally different colour which is also present on each side of the face where it covers the whole area occupied by the ears, eyes and cheeks. The illustration is of a near perfect specimen, although such animals are rare and the would-be breeder of prize-winning stock must be prepared for many disappointments before his aims are achieved, as the vast majority of Dutch Cavies have markings which by no means coincide with those of the ideal specimen. I imagine it must be rather infuriating to inspect a newly born litter containing one which would almost certainly have swept all off the show-bench before him were it not for a diminutive 'peninsular' of colour running where it ought not into the white or some other such minor blemish. As a result of this the pet market is very well supplied with mismarked Dutch, which, as a rule, are imperfect where the head is concerned, rather than round the hindquarters, or 'saddle' to be more correct.

Dutch Cavies appear in red, chocolate, black and agouti (q.v.), although those of the former colour are for some reason the most popular and plentiful, probably because red and white is such an attractive colour scheme.

The AGOUTI Cavy is so called because its colour so closely resembles that of a wild rodent, also from South America, of the same name. Briefly it may be described as having each hair banded in black, golden, and black again which gives the animal a decided 'pepper and salt' appearance, although this shade applies only to those known as Golden Agoutis for there are also varieties which are banded with 'silver' (grey) and cinnamon – colours which do not occur in the wild animal. This cinnamon, incidentally, is a clear lightish brown and is perhaps the least attractive of the three varieties.

Agouti Cavies are usually liberally sprinkled with what are known as guard hairs, which are longer than the others and wholly black, giving a generally dark appearance besides concealing the true colour. These should be removed (if you intend to show your stock they will *have* to be) either by a vigorous though careful brushing or, alternatively, by being plucked out with the fingers. I imagine this latter method to be the most satisfactory but it obviously requires more experience and should not be attempted by a novice unless he has an experienced fancier to instruct him as he goes along. In some wasters (the term used rather arrogantly to describe specimens which are imperfectly marked or otherwise not up to show standard) there are often quite large areas, usually on the sides and flanks, which are totally devoid of any ticking whatsoever and in any case the underparts are similarly clear in all specimens, of show standard or otherwise.

One of the most oddly marked of all domestic animals is surely the TORTOISESHELL Cavy which has a red and black coat marked off into very definite checks or squares, which, in a really good specimen, probably come the nearest to being straight lines in mammal markings. This is another very old variety, but appears to be losing popularity and as a result good breeding stock is by no means easy to obtain in this day and age as only a handful of people are maintaining studs of anything like size. Not a few Tortoiseshells have Tortoiseshell and White (q.v.) blood in them, which has been introduced in an attempt to bring fresh stamina from a not too far related variety into a dwindling race; this was doubtless a step in the right direction from a physiological point of view but

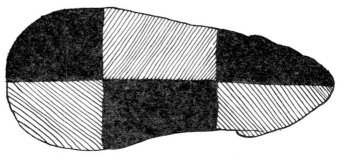

Fig. 6. Ideal markings of the Tortoiseshell Cavy.

unfortunately it has also meant that these individuals have white patches, not only in *their* coats but also in those of their offspring, and this colour is strictly taboo where Tortoiseshells are concerned. Traces of brindling in the coat is another fault which will have to bred out if it is present in one's stock although this will be by no means an easy matter as new and unrelated animals of this numerically weak race will not be easy to obtain. Fig. 12 shows a typical specimen of this quaint race.

If anything, the TORTOISESHELL AND WHITE Cavy is even more striking in appearance than the last one to come under discussion, as it is chequered with white as well as red and black and is certainly the more attractive of the two. There is no particular order in which the squares are arranged as will be seen from the illustrations, although any youngsters which appear with two squares of the same colour side by side would be useless for exhibiting with as this is a very bad fault indeed. Almost needless to say, there are a very large number of mismarked Tortoiseshell and White Cavies born. Specimens bearing perfect examples of such complicated markings are obviously rare, and as such command a high price – but the 'wasters' should be kept and bred with as they are perfectly capable of producing well marked young – markings which come up to show standard are something in the nature of an accident, it must be remembered.

Just how the ABYSSINIAN Cavy gets its name is a complete mystery, as the genus Cavia has no African associations whatsoever, in spite of which I once read an article in which someone had written to the author, a well known authority on Cavies, asking for details of their origin – to be assured by him that they came from Peru and *Abyssinia*!

This type of Cavy is unique in having its rather harsh fur arranged in very definite rosettes – four across the body, a large one on each hip and a rather smaller one placed immediately above this on the rump, while two which are smaller still are situated on the shoulders; there is also a little crest or mane and this is extended in the form of a ridge right along the back until it reaches the rump. The rosettes must be well defined and radiate from a truly minute centre and must not merge into each other, while the coat must not exceed a length of $1\frac{1}{2}$in.

Abyssinians can be bred in a wide variety of colours, although those in which they most frequently appear are Self Reds and Blacks, Golden and Silver Agoutis, Tortoiseshell, Tortoiseshell and White, and what might well be termed Skewbald and Piebald, or in other words white with red or black markings. Needless to say, Abyssinians will breed very freely with smooth haired Cavies which is why one sees so many with just an odd rosette or two dotted here and there as though the wearer were trying to make up his mind whether or not to be an Abyssinian at all, but of course these individuals are useless for showing.

Earlier I mentioned that the PERUVIAN was the most grotesque looking of all the Cavies and, frankly, I really think that one has to see a show specimen before one is willing to believe the existence of such a creature! Briefly this variety may be described as being an ordinary Cavy which has abnormally long hair – so much so that over the hindquarters it may actually measure 36 in. in some exceptional specimens; yes, one yard! The texture of the hair should be soft and silky and the whole animal must be well and truly covered, even over the head and face. There are no particular colours peculiar to the Peruvian, and practically all the known ones occur in the race, although the lighter ones appear to be rather more common for some reason or other – possibly because they are rather more attractive and therefore more likely to catch the judge's eye at a show. Rather more care is needed in the preparation of a Peruvian before a show than is usual in the case of the other varieties as the very exaggerated pelage must be very carefully groomed to ensure that there are no clots or tangles present, although regular brushing at all times will obviate the risk of this considerably. Some breeders keep their stock in curlers at all times other than when actually grooming in order to improve their coats – we all know that some people regard those who keep animals as being slightly mad; when I think of this sort of activity I am rather inclined to see their point of view!

One peculiarity of this Cavy is its tendency to chew either its own coat or those of its cage mates, which can be distinctly annoying if one wishes to show with them; this behaviour is generally regarded as being something of a mystery in its origin but offhand I would suggest that the cause is probably boredom, so it is a case of prevention being better than cure. When a sow is about to give birth to young it is nearly always advisable to clip away the fur on the underparts or the chances are that when the youngsters arrive they will be unable to derive nourishment through not being able to find and/or reach the teats through the abnormal thickness and length of the coat.

Needless to say the cage in which a Peruvian is kept must be thoroughly cleaned out very frequently or the hair will quickly become very soiled and unattractive. It is advisable to examine the hair round the anus daily as this is inclined to become impregnated with faeces and urine which will result in a very unpleasant mass which may ultimately have to be clipped away. Please, please, do not keep Peruvians unless you can devote a great deal of time to them.

CHAPTER SEVEN

The Cavy in Health and Sickness

FORTUNATELY, when compared with most domestic animals, the Cavy has few ailments likely to affect it but unfortunately, when it does fall ill, it seems completely to lose the will to live and almost invariably dies in a very short time. It is significant that out of all the Cavies I have owned only one has been 'pulled through' an illness, and I am no spare-time casual hobbyist but one who has devoted his life to animal husbandry, both wild and domestic.

Actually the Cavy is a very easy subject to keep in good health provided it is supplied with plenty of good food, dry bedding, roomy quarters and reasonable protection from cold damp weather; in fact under these conditions it should live about five years or so which is quite a long time for a small rodent. Its eyes will be full and bright, its coat 'alive' and glossy and its appetite excellent, while its movements should be rapid and almost 'clockwork mouse-like' – so much for the Cavy in good health, now let us look at a few ills which may befall it.

One of the commonest Cavy maladies appears quite inexplicable and I feel there is plenty of scope in this direction for scientific investigation into the matter; the patient falls over to on its side, or perhaps more often, sits huddled up in a listless fashion; the hair loses its bloom and is inclined to 'stand up', especially at the back of the head just where the part of the brain known as the cerebellum (which controls the body movements) is situated, and the eyes appear to be cloudy and semi-opaque. As it all seems such a nebulous matter there is little that can be done for the sufferer before, in a few hours, he dies, when the autopsy reveals nothing greatly amiss apart from a trace of bronchial pneumonia but hardly severe enough to have been fatal so quickly. There the matter appears to end, but I feel that the presence of the pneumonia is significant as this can be caused through shock (which is why one so often hears of elderly people falling, breaking limbs, and then dying in hospital some time later from this lung complaint) which might possibly suggest a severe fright such as might be caused by a sudden visitation from a cat or similar enemy; but on the other hand I have known what might almost be termed epidemics of this which have lasted for some time, making the possibilities of a whole series of inexplicable shocks highly unlikely. Of course, it is quite likely that some other fancier may have experienced similar trouble among his stock and either have arrived at some more logical conclusion or have solved the problem pathologically, in which case I would be most interested to hear from him.

During very cold weather, usually after a sudden and unexpected drop in the temperature at night, some animals may be picked up in a very distressed condition obviously suffering from exposure, especially if they have not had enough straw to burrow into for warmth. Remove the affected ones to a warm room immediately and offer (gently opening the mouth and pouring down the throat if need be) a little whiskey – an admittedly foul tasting but invaluable commodity which no livestock keeper should be without, as its medicinal properties are sometimes little short of miraculous. Infra-red lamp treatment is also very effective and its use in the indoor Caviary may prove a preventative for various Winter ills; in fact this is another piece of equipment I would not care to be without.

Too dry a diet may easily cause constipation which may culminate in prolapse of the rectum, a distressing and serious condition in which part of the colon protrudes down, in tube shape, from the anus. This needs prompt treatment from a veterinary practitioner who will probably operate, but the whole procedure is a terrific shock to the sufferer who does not often fully recover; I have known such a robust and sturdy creature as a Skunk die from delayed shock after such an operation.

Diarrhoea is often caused through a diet containing an over-abundance of greenstuff, or perhaps dirty or contaminated food; the commonest 'cure' is arrowroot offered in milk or mixed in mash, but this is merely a solidifying agent to the copious and greenish faeces which are the prime symptoms of this trouble, and does not get at the actual cause of it. There is an excellent and effective substance known as Terramycin which wreaks havoc with the bugs causing bowel infections and which I cannot praise too highly, but this is obtainable only from a veterinary surgeon who will prescribe the necessary dose. Another good, though perhaps slower, cure is to remove the sufferer to fresh quarters and change his diet completely, preferably making it a dryer one than before. Notice that I suggest removal to a new cage; as I pointed out in another book in this series*, I have never known any sick animal to recover if it remains for treatment in the cage or compartment in which it initially fell ill. Just why this is so is by no means clear, but it nevertheless appears to be an invariable rule – although doubtless at least one reader will be able to disprove it.

Sometimes two amorous boars will fight and one, or both, sustain quite badly torn ears which will have to be cleansed gently with cotton wool dipped in cold water (not warm or you will only increase the flow of blood) and then

* *Unusual Pets* (Foyle), 1958, 4s.

anointed with penicillin ointment or some such similar preparation. Really bad gashes are rare but are sometimes inflicted on the neck and sides where they run the risk of turning septic unless they are washed and regularly cleaned with T.C.P.; really severe ones, say over an inch in length, will probably need stitching. This is quite a simple matter – if you know how – if not your veterinary surgeon will make a neat job of it in a few minutes. In point of fact I would rather deal with the most badly injured Cavy patient than one which seemed only mildly 'off colour' as the chances are overwhelmingly in favour of the latter showing no definite symptoms of anything recognized 'in the book' and not responding to any treatment which might rather hopefully be given. Fortunately we have the services of an excellent veterinary surgeon who never bats an eye at some of the unlikely patients we present him with, but even he frankly admits that he is sometimes nonplussed – as any good one should if the occasion arises.

Some Cavy troubles are quite easily treated – such as skin eruptions, which can be very infectious and will soon spread in a colony unless the affected members are removed, after which the hair over the infected parts will have to be clipped away carefully with a pair of scissors and the skin massaged with any of the numerous skin ointments which are on the market, most of which contain sulphur in some shape or form. This treatment will have to be repeated at regular intervals until the cure is effected but even then it is advisable to keep the ex-patient segregated for some time until you are sure there is no risk of a recurrence.

Overgrown claws are another minor trouble, especially in animals which are normally kept on soft ground or on thick straw where their claws cannot be kept down by general wear and tear in the natural way. Hold the foot up to a strong light where the vein running along the base of the claw can clearly be seen and, with a pair of sharp nail scissors, clip off the dead tip where there is no vein – care must be taken not to cut the living part or the resulting haemorrhage may be difficult to quell.

As these animals are rodents their teeth are perpetually growing and occasionally one gets a little out of true and, having no corresponding tooth to grind on, grows at an alarming rate until it may prevent its owner from eating properly. In view of this it is a good plan to make periodic 'mouth inspections' in the Caviary and remove any requiring dental treatment. This is usually a two person 'job', one to hold both the Cavy with its mouth open (also to run the risk of an accidental nip, but who could blame the obviously terrified patient?) while the other goes into action with a nail file held in a steady hand. Most protruding teeth can be filed to their normal size in a very short time but occasionally a really overgrown one needs attention with a strong pair of nail clippers which are probably the best instruments for cutting the end off; in either case, however, the patient must be watched closely after treatment as individuals with these abnormal teeth tend to keep reverting to them – sometimes throughout their lives.

When buying a new Cavy take the trouble to examine its nose: there may be a little dried mucous round the nostrils which means it is suffering from a slight cold and, unless treated, will be dead in a few days. Point this out to the breeder who may be genuinely unaware of it; suggest to him that he puts the sufferer in a warm cage thickly carpeted with straw which has been liberally sprinkled with oil of eucalyptus (obtainable cheaply from any chemist) – he may not know of this often effective remedy and be truly grateful but there is always a sporting chance that he will ask who you are trying to teach, whereupon you should reply that if he does not know his own name how does he think you can tell him. Also run your hands over the animal of your choice to determine whether he is firm and reasonably plump; if he is not it may well be a sign of old age or possibly overgrown teeth which are preventing him from feeding properly, while one which sits listlessly with its body in almost a flattened posture and livens up only when you attempt to handle it should likewise be rejected as something will definitely be wrong.

No matter how long you have kept these attractive little animals you can, by using your powers of observation, learn something new about them almost every day. Such mental notes can, in time, be extremely valuable when you have, as all fanciers do on occasions, to combat some mysterious Cavy ailment which has suddenly reared its ugly head. In fact, as I mentioned in an earlier chapter, getting to know one's charges is one of the most vital factors in animal husbandry.

POSTSCRIPT

Since writing this book I have been working on another (on animals, of course), and, while collecting material for it in the University Museum at Manchester, I was surprised to find, tucked away in an unobtrusive corner, two mounted animals labelled 'Wild Guinea Pig. *Cavia aperea*. Brazil'. That was all, with no real information about them, but I found the creatures most interesting indeed. Mid greyish-brown in colour they were about the size of the domestic Cavy but had much more pointed, almost rat-like faces which somehow made them look rather un-Cavy like. Since then I have thought quite a lot about these animals, at first imagining that they might possibly be the illusive Restless Cavy, although if this is the case it would appear that their domestic successors have undergone a remarkable head change; could our familiar pets be the result of a hybridization between this and some other closely related species? Your guess is as good as mine.

Index